THE 300-MILE MAN
Roberto Marron Doubles Tuscobia's Winter Ultra 150

by Phillip Gary Smith

Other Books by Phillip Gary Smith

Ultra Superior

HARMONIZING: Keys to Living in the Song of Life

Copyright © 2013 Ultra Superior Media
All rights reserved
ISBN-10: 0615911722
ISBN-13: 978-0615911724
Ultra Superior Media

To those who endure, yet persevere, on trails
and in life by responding to the edict
"Never Give Up."

Contents

Tuscobia and similar ultra distance races do not use mile-markers. They have checkpoints (aid stations) often with great distances between them. Honoring that, this book has checkpoints as chapters without page numbers.

HAPPY NEW YEAR, MAN
CHECKPOINT ONE

"Come, gentlemen, I hope we shall drink down any unkindness." William Shakespeare

"THIS IS THE POLICE! I WANT TO SEE YOUR HANDS!"

Roberto Marron's 2013 New Year's morning comes unexpectedly alive like a shooting star over the frigid Tuscobia Trail. Stretched out in snowy northern Wisconsin, his sleeping bag rated to -40 degrees surrounding him like an insulated cocoon, he groggily thinks, "It's New Year's, man. What is this? I'm just sleeping."

The county sheriff wasn't in a celebratory mood either at daybreak. Marron lay deep, a baklava protecting his face. Just turning to see who provided his harsh wake-up becomes effort. The bag was positioned in such a way he had to lift his head back over his shoulder just to get a glimpse.

The officer's suspicions were aroused when earlier he patrolled by, noticing a parked silver Chrysler PT Cruiser. He checks again later, the car is gone. In its place there is a body lying prone near the road.

That's a possible dead man, he reasoned. Out loud, he calls to the very still bag, questioning, hoping for a response. A good first question for any law enforcement isn't "Are you alive?" or "Do you need help?" Rather, the first question should be just as he asked: "Do you have a weapon?"

Roberto Marron self-portrait

Marron began to think his outlandish idea of doubling the 150-mile Tuscobia Winter Ultra run, immediately repeating the race course just finished Sunday, might need reconsideration. This is happening early Tuesday, the first day of 2013 but the second day in his quest to complete 300 miles racing and trekking on Tuscobia's snow-covered trails.

"No," he responds, answering the officer's question, speaking in his staccato Spanish inflection, one not generally heard in that area particularly in the dead of winter while in the middle of nowhere. He pulled his empty hands from the comfortable oven provided by the bag, exposing them up to the frigid air and the officer.

The county sheriff continued his quest exclaiming, "Explain what you're doing here, and show me some ID now!"

Lying flat in the snow, Marron faces potentially dire trouble for something of which he knows nothing. He finds himself in this situation when just three short years ago he entered the very first 150 mile Tuscobia Winter Ultra for runners. That was 2010.

TUSCOLA
CHECKPOINT TWO

"An Indian respects a brave man, but he despises a coward"
Hin-mah-too-yah-lat-kekt known as Chief Joseph (1840-1904)

The Tuscobia Winter Ultras began with the idea of utilizing the 74 miles of Tuscobia trail reclaimed from the old Tuscobia Railroad whose operations formed in 1914. The name is likely derived from an American Indian word "Tuscola" translating to level flat land just like this terrain. The rail was known as the Omaha Line from ownership stemming to the Omaha Railway Company. Later, it came under control of the Chicago and Northwestern Railway. They renamed the rail as the Park Falls Line. The conversion to its present uses as a recreation trail connecting parks and towns along its distance emerged in 1968.

The event, originally founded by Tim Roe, Winter, Wis., celebrates the trail in winter's surprise. Snowbikers, cross-country skiers and runners gather to navigate either the full-trail 75 miles (transportation to the start, finishing at the trailhead), an out-and-back 150 miles or a taste, just 35 miles as a slice of trail. The 150 starts and ends in Park Falls, the hometown of Tuscobia Winter Ultras. The others provide rousing bus rides to the respective starting points, mostly a westerly direction, and race back to Park Falls.

One way from the trail's far western end at Rice Lake meanders East/Northeast, passing through the Flambeau State Forest and Chequamegon National Forest before reaching Park Falls.

Flambeau River State Forest is formed around the confluence of the North and South Forks of the river providing approximately 92 miles of wilderness waterways between the two. The northern fork, the longest fork in the state forest at 77 miles, is considered more tranquil while its southern brother resembles a tempest. The park station is located in Winter where a key checkpoint in the Tuscobia ultra services racers traveling in both directions.

Eventually the Flambeau River meanders into the Chippewa, near Chippewa Falls, before becoming one of ten that reach as their destination the mighty Mississippi River.

The Chequamegon National Forest is now the Chequamegon-Nicolet National Forest. In 1993 the US Forest Service combined management of the two as a natural cost-savings move. In 1933 both were preserved independently for 60 years. As one indication of the lack of density in this region, there are five wilderness areas between the 1 1/2 million acres these two national forests inhabit. Their headquarters are in Park Falls, population pushing 2500. The Flambeau River dissects the city into two halves as the southwest flow, originating twenty plus miles away at a northeast angle, suddenly turns southerly just as if such a setup could be planned. The river bends westerly again practically at the city limits.

Surrounded by covered bridges, the rapid flows below the lower dam capture the Flambeau's power and reflect the ambition showing in the town's motto Bridging Nature with Industry. The trailhead of Tuscobia opens wide to welcome the ambitious to tour its historic route on the town's westside. Several city blocks east from the trailhead locate the race's finish line at Chequamegon Canoe Club (CCC) on a western corner of the main drag, Highway 13, near the center of town. Built inside an ancient, old-time but small lumberjack hotel, and it still has that feel, one instantly blends in its dark corners and few booths, finding scattered chairs to plop down. A musician plays live next to the bar with surprising intensity.

Order Cheesehead Shepherds Pie, Brisket & Spuds--this is potato land, too--while celebrating their theme "Oui du Wisconsin." Indeed, that's Wisconsin! Just be careful not to mix "oui" with OUI, a designation of driving impaired, "operating under the influence." CCC is a quaint, rustic, and thoroughly unique Wisconsin-style bistro, perfect for Tuscobia's appeal to the edge, uncommon, non-normal.

FROSTBITE FALLS
CHECKPOINT THREE

"I got three whippings a day from my mama."
Evander Holyfield

In 2011 new race directors, well-known Midwest ultra trail racers Helen Lavin and Chris Scotch, now Mr. and Mrs. Scotch, assumed control of the Tuscobia Winter Ultras. One of their first acts was to stretch the 50 km distance to a 35-mile race by moving the start about five miles further west on the trail to Ojibwa from Winter. The Tuscobia 150 creates a true companion race for the granddaddy of U.S. continental winter ultras, the Arrowhead 135 staged in northern Minnesota. The well-known Badwater 135 challenges a parched desert endured in Death Valley as the marquee summer endurance event; Arrowhead is winter's frigid reply.

Four signed on to attempt the snowy inaugural 150-mile run in 2010, the longest such race designed for snow in the continental U.S. The number ticked to six entrants in 2011. Only Scotch and Marron completed the entire trail of Tuscobia by running in its two years of competition prior to 2012's December race. Marron possessed no winter racing experience at the time. The demands of Tuscobia are unique with long, straight, hypnotic trails lined by forests from the former railroad bed producing a mentally tough layout. Why would he enter the first year's event cold? "I'm trying to qualify for Arrowhead; this will do it." Arrowhead starts at the nation's ice box, International Falls, also known as Frostbite Falls. The trail meanders a southerly route on what woodsmen recall as the Capekona Trace.

Competitors may face extreme cold or raging snow coupled with a lonesome journey broken only by distant checkpoints. Winter ultra distance races are as far from big city marathons, with their aid stations, bands and applauding onlookers every mile, as a northern winter is from an Arizona summer. Marron's first Arrowhead attempt, Monday, January 31, 2011, gave him a whipping that ended in disappointment. Arrowhead saved its tricks that year—gelid air—for the overnight. Unofficial gauges registered lows plummeting to -40 degrees. Marron's thermos cap froze solid to the container though the liquid inside didn't. Still, what

good was it? He couldn't drink it. Dehydration attacks in extreme cold just as in extreme heat. Effects of fatigue, weakness in muscles, poor concentration and mental acumen, and then slowing metabolism all affect one's mood, the ability to function. You're in trouble yet can't think how to escape it. Add the deliberateness one has to use in bitter cold to do anything, even the smallest task, and the opportunity for failure increases dynamically.

"I tried to melt snow with my fancy stove I had bought" he explained. "It wouldn't turn on" ending his ability to get liquids. He promptly returned the stove for a refund when he arrived home. "Bad clothes," he described, also affected his attempt as he soaked in body sweat that then froze. He did not have the technical clothing to minimize that threat. The attempt doomed, Marron admitted, "I'm dehydrated; I could go no more."

"I was frustrated with myself; why didn't I bring different gear?" On the course, "Double socks didn't work; it felt like fire on the bottoms. I feared frostbite. I changed to insulation boots, but (on the) second night it was worse. The first day I was wearing running shoes. The boots were worse because the insulation added heat; changed back to running shoes, but then freezing. Then I tried boot without socks that were worse. I was trying to figure out what to do."

Those feet required nearly two months to recover.

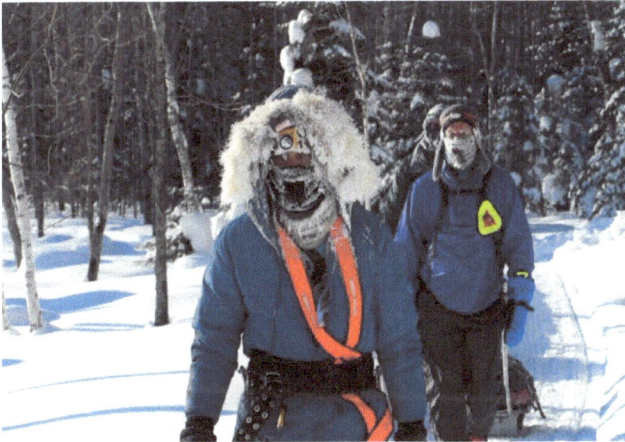

Endurance athletes making way during the frigidly difficult 2011 Arrowhead

Early Wednesday a snowmobile sweep, those patrols checking trails for problems like competitors in peril or missing markers on the trail, happened by. Climbing on that machine ended his first Arrowhead attempt after completing an estimated 99 miles.

FOOL
CHECKPOINT FOUR

"It's-A-Real-Hard-Race." John Storkamp 3-time Arrowhead winner coolly describing why he didn't finish 3 times

Marron's second Arrowhead race, one year later, started Monday morning January 30, 2012. At 7:04--four minutes after the snowbikes and two minutes after the skiers--the foot racers are off. Scooting by the Voyageurs National Park, Marron enters the first checkpoint, Gateway General Store, Kabetogama, literally the entry to the park, after his first twelve hours on the trails. That's about 40 miles.

While Gateway acts as something akin to a city hall and recreation venue for the community, it's major hurrah is as the main entrance to Voyageurs. This National Park established in 1975 stands as Minnesota's only one, lying as the National Park Service calls "the heart of the North American Continent." The well-known Smoky Mountains likely has more visitors in one week than Voyageurs in one year, but that is just one of the coveted features of the country's only water-based park.

Originally fur trading, logging, mining and commercial fishing dominated the area. A gold rush overcame the area in mid-1893; the story is told on the park's Little American Island.

Unique in today's world, many visitor destinations are only accessed by boat. Also notable is the rock statuary of the Ellsworth Rock Gardens. The only hotel on the property, The Kettle Falls, whose accessibility is limited to water, sits near naturally enough the Kettle Falls Dam. A history filled with ribaldry, the lodge now serves comfort foods and warm hospitality.

Marron steps out in the dark, 8:17 p.m., to spend the overnight and morning pulling his pulk through a long and lonesome night to the next step in completing Arrowhead.

He reaches MelGeo, about 30 miles further, the shorthand for Melgeorges Elephant Lake Lodge, Orr, for the second time in his life. It's 16 hours later at 12:15 p.m. Tuesday; he is now a little more than halfway done. The lake famous for its bounty of Minnesota's contribution to the species of freshwater

Walleye fish, also hosts one of the more unique winter events in the country: An antique snowmobile race with an antique division, classic division and vintage division. The oldest snowmobile winning a medal went to local enthusiast, Jacob Holman's 1960 Polaris Autoboggin that sported a rear engine and something more than 9 horsepower.

1960 KE-95

MelGeo marks a change in the terrain; the trails to this point are relatively flat, enjoyable but in the conditions always a challenge. Making way to the next checkpoint, SkiPulk, approximately 40 miles further south, the word rugged becomes the norm. Huge exposed rock, boulders and debris represent some of the oldest volcanic activity on the globe, now wearing down after nature's attack of glaciers and the annual four seasons of change. It is now Wednesday. Marron arrives at the trailside SkiPulk tent (mile 111) near Cook's Winnifred Road just before 8:00 a.m. after roughly a 20-hour stretch on the trail. Shortly, he zipped out to claim one dream, an Arrowhead 135 finish. It's midafternoon, Wednesday, the race accomplished in 56:51, three hours to spare, 21st of 50 entrants. 28 completed the entire distance.

Jason Buffington, Duluth, Minn., won in a record 37 hours, 16 minutes; wow! Parker Rios, Brookfield, Wis., took second 3 1/2 hours later. Rios won the heavy-snow-fest that marked the 2013 version in 45 hours, a feat that at least equals Buffington's accomplishment.

Marron posses a strong mind-over-matter composure, like all of these ultra athletes do, which will pay off later in his biggest adventure yet. But it is important to realize accomplishing these individual finishes are Herculean experiences requiring extreme athletes. Racers drag a 40-pound pulk, a specialized carrier sled, the entire distance packed with survival gear, food, and clothing while traversing hills and trails. Experiencing temperature extremes and conditions oftentimes accompanied by heavy snows and bitter winds challenging their bodies is testament enough to their willpower and fortitude.

It is also a test of securing the proper gear beyond the requirements. The compulsory gear and rules for Arrowhead read something like a list of fear factors in a prospectus, except it is not legal talk coming at you. These are voices of experience. For example, regarding the need of a -20 degree sleeping bag, the race notes: "If you skimp here you are foolish. And we will not allow you to skimp. So, do not skimp. Fool. 2011 it was -42 degrees on trail."

If you fail a cutoff or are pulled from the race for your own safety, the following caution will get your attention: "If you don't stop after failing to meet checkpoint cutoff you will be firmly spanked and banned from future Arrowheads."

Why, you may ask, do racers need flashing LED lights front and back, the more the better? "Keep on all the time. Highly important . . . this may well prevent you from being (a) hood ornament on large fast-moving snowmachines."

You wear a whistle to call for help because "your mouth is too numb to yell."

With a required 3,000 calories as an emergency supply at all times, including when reaching the finish, along with each day's food supply probably equating to more than 6,000, a racer can easily be sporting 10,000 calories on the trails.

In case one wonders, a large family-sized bag of Doritos tops out, before dips by the way, at around 2,000 calories. The Arrowhead website suggests a jar of peanut butter or a pound of butter as the component for the emergency supply.

If stuck in a tent, a blizzard blowing by while all hunkered down . . . I'm thinking more Doritos.

Consider the experience of ultra trail veteran John Storkamp, Hastings, Minn., a three-time winner of Arrowhead out of eight prior starts. He has tallied five finishes, which include the three gold, a bronze, and then a silver finish in the brutal

Arrowhead Expert, John Storkamp, wins the 2012 Tuscobia

January, 2013 edition. That means he did not finish (DNF) three times including 2012. Why, I asked him, does such an expert at this event not finish. His succinct answer says it all. "It-is-a-real-hard-race."

GITCHE GUMEE
CHECKPOINT FIVE

"In the fields of observation chance favors only the prepared mind." Louis Pasteur

Marron abides by this command: "Whatever you think is what your body will do. Think you will drop, you will drop. Think you can run, you can run." He takes favorite DVDs on these trips to watch while prepping for the race, tough titles like "Gladiator" and "Black Hawk Down."

Without possessing a strong mindset like ultra endurance athletes Storkamp, Marron and the others in this tome who toe the start for one of these behemoths, one can never seriously consider participating in extreme endurance challenges. Racers can go a long way in training plus test one's ability with mileages like the 35-mile option at Tuscobia or the 50-mile Superior Trail challenge, but these extreme events, the basis of this book . . . the harsh reality of them is more difficult than one can conceive.

Marron began to develop his hardcore determination as a young man deep in Mexico's forests where he lived before arriving Minnesota in 2005. Neither a smoker nor drinker, "I joined the Mexican Army in 1993. I wanted to be a part of the Special Forces elite Grupo Aeromóvil de Fuerzas Especiales (Special Forces Airmobile Group, GAFE). You had to be an officer to join, but in 1994 (the military) needed more because of domestic problems. That's when I raised my hand. My trainer was a U.S. Green Beret."

Four hundred and twenty signed up; 68 passed the finals. Then after the last cut, a horrendously tough "four months of training, 22 passed. I was one of those. I was also a police officer starting later in 2005."

He strengthened his resolve and trail conditioning by completing both the 2011 and 2012 Superior 100 Trail Races, one of the United States' top-10, and one of the most difficult, trail events. Part of the allure of Superior occurs at night where the black of darkness kills vision; spare lights are a necessity.

Raced on the Superior Hiking Trails bordering Lake Superior, these trails are rough, rooty and most times rocky. They eat quadriceps like kids with candy mints. The elite runners finish this kingpin of Wilderness Athlete's Gnarly Bandit Ultra Trail Series under 24 hours, but many push its cutoff of 38 hours if they get that far.

It is seriously hard. Storkamp, the race director of this and a portfolio of top endurance trail events, terms it "rugged, relentless and remote." Begun in 1991, the race became one of the earliest 100-mile events in the country. As a bonus, the natural trails make the actual distance traveled 103 miles. The event's history yields it legacy and legendary status.

A competitor dwells with Longfellow's "The Song of Hiawatha" while traipsing the Superior Forest trails skirting the world's largest inland freshwater ocean, Lake Superior. Best known of his epic are the 94; 94-lines making infamous "By the shores of Gitche Gumee/by the shining Big-Sea-Water/Dark behind it rose the forest/Rose the black and gloomy pine-trees/Rose the firs with cones upon them . . . . "

TUSCOBIA OUT
CHECKPOINT SIX

"The beginning is always today."
Mary Shelley (writer/novelist 1797-1851)

A group of nine gathered at the CCC for the start of the 2012 150-mile foot-version of Tuscobia—seven men, two women—on Friday, just three days after Christmas. Another eight events of running, skiing and snowbiking at distances of 150, 75 and 35 miles depart at various times over the weekend before everything wraps up for official times Sunday night at 6:00 p.m.

The 6:00 a.m. start earns a police escort from the CCC backdoor Tuscobia tent, complete with white lights stringing its outline, to the trailhead some half-mile away. No hoopla, no bands; just nine ambitious endurance athletes pursuing a challenge.

One competitor—Marron—announced a shocking goal the night before: he is going to attempt a double-150. Finish the race, then turn around and cover his same tracks for another 150, a breathtaking 300 miles while pulling his lifeline, the sled pulk, behind him the entire way. The Tuscobia 75 and 150-mile races and Arrowhead, too, are semi-supported meaning food, beverages and drop bags are at distant checkpoints. Competitors can buy anything from restaurants, gas stations and so on during the race, "but there is not to be any other outside help, crews, or pacers," the rules dictate, though racers may assist other racers. In other words . . . you're on your own.

Marron arrived at the first checkpoint in the tiny town of Winter—named in honor of a railroad official, John Winter—30 miles out at 1:50 p.m., just under eight hours into the contest. Pulling with him came Logan Polfuss, the race's youngest competitor in any class at 17, both eating heartily from the teen's seemingly endless supply of Fritos. Living in Pickett, near Oshkosh, Polfuss has a surprising ultra background for one under the age of 20. He completed 2012's Kettle Moraine 100 mile, one of five races chosen for the Wilderness Athlete's Gnarly Bandit Ultra Trail Series. He debated whether to race the 75 or 150, but fate determined his choice as the simpler distance filled quickly. Perhaps destiny awarded him instead an amazing experience, a lifetime adventure for his first winter ultra distance challenge.

Alicia Hudelson, 2012's first-place woman at the Arrowhead 135, zoomed out of Winter at 1:15 p.m. with the early overall lead. Storkamp and Matt Long--who had captured third place in 2012's Arrowhead--followed. After a 45-minute refresher, Marron and Polfuss leave along with Scotch at 2:35 p.m. Saturday afternoon. Hudelson, while in the lead, dropped 33 miles later when entering the second checkpoint, Birchwood, just before midnight. Watch for her in future winter ultras. The finish in 2012 at Arrowhead, 2009's second place at the Wild Duluth 100 km trail race--a race that runs like a 100 miles--and a 31-hour Superior 100 finish in September, 2013, proves she is the real deal.

Highly experienced ultra runner Lynn Saari struggled in to Birchwood much later, pulling out of the event. She had completed the Ozark Trail 100 early in November before Tuscobia plus has multiple finishes at the Zumbro Endurance 100 mile event near her home in Rochester, Minn. with ultra distance husband, Daryl. They are entered together in the 2013 Tuscobia 150-mile snowbike division

Chuck Fritz of central Iowa became Tuscobia's first casualty. "I made it out of Winter. I dropped at (the BP Food Mart) convenience store in Ojibwa" approximately six miles further but never crossing the mostly frozen Chippewa River. "I went into the store to get hot chocolate, and while I was in there my race fell apart mentally. . . (I) caught a ride back to Winter, eventually making it to the start line," his Tuscobia race done. Fritz is no amateur (see next photo, competing in a

2011 Kansas Ultra). "I finished the Leadville Trail 100 in 2011, and although the races are very different, I'd say a winter ultra is more difficult. Winter ultras require more gear, impose more isolation, and there are just more variables that can go the wrong way."

"I really enjoyed the challenge in Wisconsin," he said. "I'm a former Marine Corps sergeant, and I've got a couple of Boston's under my belt, 2011 and 2012. In a manner of speaking Boston is to Leadville as Leadville is to Tuscobia."
He updated me that he finished the dramatic 2013 Boston-bombed race while his wife and daughters were there with him. They were sitting safely in a cafe when the terrorists struck. The lure of Tuscobia doesn't just disappear. Fritz said, "It was my first winter ultra, and I plan to return to Park Falls (in 2013) to compete again and finish with better gear and preparation."

After Hudelson's drop, the new leaders became Storkamp and Long. At the Birchwood aid station before midnight, the duo were already gone for more than an hour when Marron arrived at 1:42 Saturday morning, minutes ahead of Polfuss. Six remain in the 150 as Polfuss leaves at 2:40 a.m. quickly followed by Marron, Scotch then Taylor.

2011 ...to Run

ISN'T THAT NICE
CHECKPOINT SEVEN

"Please; cut the fuse." Herrera pleading with Pike Bishop (William Holden) in "The Wild Bunch"

The Tuscobia Trail terminates at Rice Lake, 12 1/2 miles further west after leaving Birchwood's aid. One thinks: "I've got to go out for 12 1/2 miles and then come right back here another 12 1/2 miles to end just where I'm standing now," the runner's dirge at an out-and-back course.

The 75-mile return trip along these same trails looms large for the half-dozen foot-racers rounding the turn. Back to Birchwood, adding a near-marathon distance to their totals since they were last there, Long and Storkamp scoot out, heading in minutes before 11:00 a.m. Saturday morning, knowing that in less than a day they'll finish. But therein lies the rub; there's an entire overnight to master again, to overcome, without mentioning the remaining distance. Scotch takes off 20 minutes later, Marron in the noon hour, Polfuss an hour past that. Taylor leaves mid-afternoon.

The last checkpoint heading in, Winter, stretches 30 miles from Tuscobia's finishing banners, nine or more hours away. The distance becomes brutally longer for some of those remaining like Taylor who clocked in at Winter just before 6:00 a.m. Sunday after pulling more than 14 hours on the trail since leaving Birchwood. He pulled on his extensive 100-mile experiences as one of the 2012 Wilderness Athlete Gnarly Bandit Ultra Series winners to bravely capture his finish after a full day racing, 8:28 p.m. Sunday evening, wrapping-up the race weekend. And proving the edict, never give up.

Storkamp has command of the lead (he slept only 5-minute naps while on the trail) leaving for his finish roughly an hour ahead of Long at 10:30 p.m. Saturday night. Scotch is out the door at 3:40 a.m. They win 1-2-3 in that order.

Solitary is the word; Storkamp treks Tuscobia's long trails

Storkamp made the Park Falls finish at 7:19 a.m. Sunday morning. Long crossed at 8:35 a.m. with Scotch at 1:49 p.m.

"Eight miles before Winter," about 112 miles into the 150 mile race while having spent hours in the dark Marron concludes, "I need to stop and rest. I felt something, sleepy, aching but found something telling me to get to the checkpoint. Hallucinations happened causing me to wander and weave from the center of the trail." Marron makes the Winter station at 2:52 a.m.

The five hours he spent there included a much needed sleep. "I knew I need water, change clothes, sleep a couple of hours first."

Marron prepares for these events, like all strong endurance competitors, with a thoughtful strategy. "Before any race, I think about what I can do when I'm (back) home, when I'm holding my baby. I imagine I'm on the trail, so I decide everything (like) food, gear, training. Once I break down everything, then I test. On the trail, I try to follow my strategy, but if gear not working so well or the body isn't responding as I expected I start to correct my strategy."

Logan, seriously considering ending his race, entered the Winter station a few minutes after 5:00 a.m. Sunday morning. "I was thinking about dropping in the past several miles, but when I woke up and saw Roberto leaving, I had to join him. I saw him do amazing finishes at Kettle and last year's Tuscobia. He was all excited since we had about nine and a half-hours to finish." Marron's enthusiasm boosts Polfuss to his finish.

Scotch left earlier as they slept. "Logan was there when I woke," recalled Marron, "We're tied at fourth. John Taylor was on the floor resting. I wanted him to come along. 'Come on,' I said. He said, 'I'm tired.'"

With that sleep energizing him, Marron heads toward the finish moments before 8:00 a.m. while Polfuss manages to get out the door about 14 minutes earlier. Soon they're back together. They share one stunning incident before the Pine Creek Road crossing. Marron explains, "We waited for one another" eating Fritos, running and walking. Then, "We (both) had to go to the bathroom (about) 12 miles before the finish." They move off the side of the trail, taking the time required to get the bundles of clothes unzipped and off for this major undertaking. And what happens? Snowbiker, Sveta Kovalchuk, the women's 150-mile winner-to-be, passes by heading to the finish. She quips to them, "Isn't that nice," then, "It's okay, it's okay."

Polfuss grins, "We couldn't help but laugh, and Roberto kept saying 'Man; that was a girl! I can't believe that was a girl!'"

Even though the two came to the trailhead on Park Falls together, Marron explained, "This is a race; so we race from that point to the finish" with Polfuss crossing first for his inaugural winter ultra, a big one at that.

Marron's bigger goal was next.

THE TUSCOBIA DOUBLE
CHECKPOINT EIGHT

"Endurance is patience concentrated."
Thomas Carlyle (Philosopher 1795-1881)

"I wanted to be the first to do the 300-mile double. I thought maybe Chris Scotch would be the first, but I wanted to as a validation. My plan to get in, call home, reorganize gear but at the finish John (Storkamp), Tony Oveson (who is to play a surprising role in the double), Helen and Chris are all there on the finish. I'm tired, but I want to wait for John Taylor. I walked up and met him (at the trailhead)." It is almost 9:00 p.m. at that point.

Oveson observed, "I didn't think he was going to (attempt the double) since he looked so beat up. From my perspective he really would have rather not have done it at that instant, but since everyone asked him, he said I'm going to do it, I'm going to do it."

"I needed some privacy," Marron explained, "(So I) went to my Mason Motel, arranged gear until 1 a.m. like switching sleds (to the longer one) to carry more gear. I used Desitin on chafing I had on legs; it worked. The alarm I set for 8:00 a.m. I went to the breakfast, seven already there talking about the race" all had completed Sunday. Marron orders hash brown potatoes, steak, French toast, a lot of coffee . . . then doubled the order with another entire serving.

Did he ever question his idea of attempting the distance again for the double? "Always my mind was focused on doing the second 150, and take four days (to complete it)."

Polfuss was astonished. "After we finished (on Sunday night) we were all hanging around the table at the CCC talking and telling stories. When Chris Scotch asked Roberto how he feels about another 'set,' I realized he was doing another 150.

(Monday morning) we all met at a local diner, and he was all smiles and running around. He went back to his motel to get ready to leave. I was shocked. I couldn't imagine doing the 150 all by yourself."

Marron left his compact wagon at the Mason Motel. "They would start it for me. I got water, filled bottles and left exactly (at) noon. It took 15 minutes to the trailhead." The saga of the second 150-mile trek, the second half of 300 on the Tuscobia Trails, began.

Marron is a master at self-talk, the mental work required to overcome obstacles and doubt, a process known well to champions. "I feel the Tuscobia 150 is mentally tough," he said, because of the long and straight distances stretching out ahead on this trail. The hardest section of an out-and-back layout is just after the turn, particularly when the trail is deteriorating in the sun even though temperatures were cold. The adrenalin of making that point is gone, only to be replaced with the realization of the distance left to be travelled. Coaching himself, he repeated, "I wanted to do this from summer, and this is the only way I can come back . . . by myself."

Oveson went to Logan's truck where stored were more bags of Fritos. "I want to be there on the second 150," Oveson decided. "In my mind I wanted to stay and help." Already repacked, he took off in pursuit of Marron "to the to Pine

Creek road where the aid station was" about 11 miles away. Jeff Allen and his wife worked this checkpoint over the weekend with a big flaming fire while serving hot cheese quesadillas. Now there were just ashes in the fire pit.

Later in the afternoon, Marron hears a horn honk. "It was Tony! He wanted to be with me for a couple days."

Tony Oveson on the trail with Roberto Marron, who shows his fatigue during the second 150-mile trudge.

"My joke was," Oveson quipped, "What would you think of a Spanish guy knocking on your door asking for a ride?"

Marron arrived once again at Winter, stopping at a diner this time, the aid station long closed and cleared out. Now nearly midnight on New Year's Eve, he celebrated with hot pizza—medium with everything—and Pepsi. The waitress asked, "Are you a snowmobiler?"

The temperature slipped to -13 degrees. He trudged on to Ojibwa, about 5 1/2 miles further, arriving after 2:00 a.m. "I was cold and couldn't find the campground I knew. Looking for the shelter, can't find it, but then thinking, why do I need the shelter?"

Why, indeed; his sleeping bag and pad are enough, so he chooses to sleep out under the bright Tuscobia stars. He was hunting for Ojibwa Park, the new starting point for 2013's 35-mile race, a good change for the event. The park's entrance is slightly east of the previous race start, connecting to the main trail with a spur. Marron very likely passed right by the sign indicating the spur; those things are easy to miss at night, much less after the cumulative distance he had covered.

"I stopped and cleared the site to grass; had two trekking poles that I stuck in the snow with reflectors and lights. Laid waterproof material (a poncho-like thermal rest) and set the alarm for 7:30; planned four hours sleep with 30 minutes to pack gear." Oveson finds him and then leaves, parking his silver PT cruiser back in the small town for his sleep. Early the next morning, "I showed back up again, saw the officer and got out to explain Roberto's 300 miles, and that I had finished the official race Sunday."

"You tell me you're 65, and now you're out here running?" the surprised officer answered. "You're crazy."

Oveson didn't argue with that sentiment, but asked, "If it's okay, I'll take his ID. I got it and took it back. Then I said, 'Roberto, Happy New Year!' We rested in the car with hot coffee, pepperoni pizza and two sandwiches, our New Year's breakfast."

Thirteen hours later near 9:40 p.m., Marron makes Birchwood where the second aid station would have been. His sled experiences trouble as four holes in the frame are dragging in snow like scoops, adding weight. As a result of the more-difficult pull, his left calf is cramping.

Once again they seek out burritos at the gas station. Oveson asked if they could stay overnight on the property. They told him, "Yes, just don't park next to the building since they'll think you're robbing us. Both of us slept outside, not in the car but on the snow."

"Hey! This is the police," the squad car arriving; two sheriff deputies perch on top of them with weapons drawn. What happened, Oveson said, "Somebody goes by and sees two bodies on the ground and called 911. The Barron County Deputies arrived. They checked everything all out."
Two nights, two police encounters.

Wednesday morning at 7:30 a.m. the station opens. Naturally, they get burritos. Marron heads out to the Rice Lake turnaround where Oveson meets him, this time with hamburgers.

RADISSON
CHECKPOINT NINE

"Rose-colored glasses are never made in bifocals because nobody wants to red the small print in dreams."
Ann Landers (1918-2002)

As Marron passed a buffalo farm roaming with animals alongside the trail, he recounts his plan to make Birchwood, the first aid station going in when the race was on. It's late afternoon, a need for more self-talk since no one else is there to do it. "I always told myself I'd finish; it will be easier after the turn."

Endurance athletes work to find little positives, like this will be easier after the turn, even if they're not true. Often on the trail, you have to lie to yourself. Yes, the distance is less, but there will be new challenges to the mind, self-imposed time pressures. Little positives help the psyche endure. It helps one to make friends with their misery, wrapping arms around it, embracing the wear and tear, displaying it like a sash across the chest shouting "Misery is my Friend!"

Social media adds a whole new dimension as live-tracking in races and photos of the terrain by the competitors light up the "likes," comments and tweets, too. "I checked my FaceBook. It was good to know that people were tracking," Marron said. In between his update posts, questions compounded online such as "Anyone heard anything?" "Where is he now?" His outlandish goal became everyone's experience.

Arriving Birchwood, he was slowing. The two ate again at the same restaurant. Oveson, chatting with the waitress, explained Marron's goal. "She thought it was cool."

Only 20 percent of the distance remaining, 62 1/2 miles to go. It became painfully obvious to Marron that he would not be back before Thursday morning. He had to call Quyen, his supportive wife. She needed to take another day off from her job to tend to their little son, the pride and joy. "Made me feel happy" to talk with her, but he had to push anyway just to be back in St. Paul—a five-hour drive away—on Friday morning at 6:30 a.m.

Oveson planned to meet him at the town of Couderay, famous as one of Al Capone's secret hideouts. Oveson explained, "I told him I'm at Couderay, but Roberto said 'I can't go no more.' You're only two or three miles away I told him, and he made it about one hour."

"I was so tired," Marron explained. "I told my wife, I had to stop and sleep, but Tony motivated me to push on." About 2:00 a.m. Thursday, his body gave him no choice. "I have to sleep." With the police encounters, the duo slept inside the car covered with a stack of Oveson's blankets. On the trail by 8:00 a.m. he tried "picking up the pace to make the deadline."

Marron tests his veracity, making a self-appraisal. "Sometimes I feel, man, I think it's getting hard; once I finish I don't need to do this any more. But I think of the finish line. Then afterward I get to buy myself something, like I'm hungry when I finish. I wanna go to the restaurant and eat a lot of food. When I'm tired, I'm imagining going to sleep for two days; of course, that never happens."

Now arriving at the small town of Radisson, named after Pierre-Esprit Radisson the French explorer and trader—the namesake of the Radisson Hotels, too—Marron enjoys more nutritious burritos and meets yet another sheriff, "but very friendly; he shook my hand."

"I was feeling the pressure of time," hustling to make Winter in early afternoon. Getting hot, he peels off layers. "He was wet because he was working so hard" noted Oveson. Not stopping, Marron's traveling aid station caught up with him bringing more pizza and Mountain Dew, his cornerstones of any nutritious meal. On the trail, one eats anything-- anything--that keeps energy, mood and momentum going forward. What that is varies as greatly as the shoes and clothes these athletes wear. If you make the finish line, it worked.

CROSSING 70
CHECKPOINT TEN

*"All I want is to enter my house justified." Steve Judd
(Joel McCrea) in Peckinpah's "Ride the High Country"*

Entering tiny Draper six miles East of the little town of Winter, just past the frozen Loretta Lake, it's a dark 4:00 p.m. Thursday afternoon, now January 3rd. There the Tuscobia Trail crosses to the north side of Highway 70, a key milestone on these trails. Instead of paralleling the road, one enters a long stretch of trails with deep, quiet woods wrapping both sides like a tunnel. At night it is something akin to moving in a black pipe. Nineteen miles now remain for Marron to complete the double-distance. The time clicking on his wife's clock left no room to coast, to enjoy. The pressure builds, an ironic reward after trudging these paths seven days.

You would think a finish like in a television commercial one is leaping through the wind, bright colors flashing, traveling at the speed of sound, magically done, ready to go out for the night, now fresh as a new fallen pine cone. Untrue.

As winds pick up from the west now, it's really dark, oppressive. Oveson brought even more pizza and "Dew," encouraging Marron with small talk. "The wind will push you to the next meeting point" at Pine Creek Road when only 11 miles would remain. It's not far, it's double-ones.

Marron notices company on the trails. "I saw tracks where wolves were 2-by-2 hunting while I'm eating my turkey." Wolves would like turkey. With that, he chucked the sandwich, turned and headed in finally reaching the last segment to be done. "Roberto had stopped there for about 45 minutes," Oveson remembered, "Eating more pizza and two croissants, then jogging and walking at a fast pace" while pulling his friend, the pulk; always there, the sled with lights blinking merrily, keeping him company every step of the way.

Oveson dashed to the CCC to tell them a finish was in the cards, then backtracked on the trail several miles--pulling his own sled like any endurance racer would do--to accompany Marron traveling in.

Did he need to pull his own pulk to meet Marron? Probably not, but the thought of not taking it on the trail would never have occurred to him. It's somewhat related to wearing a seatbelt. One is accustomed to it; it is just what you do.

Finishing, Marron didn't celebrate; he couldn't. No time. Besides, the CCC had closed, the clock showed 11:25 p.m., a Thursday night. Park Falls had completed its day.

"Mentally I was tired," Marron said in classic understatement. "At the trailhead, I felt more relief" than anything. Having a deadline, pressures for a cutoff or needing to get home twists the fun of these endurance events, replacing it with a type of strenuous work. These circumstances wear on the runner. After getting the car, packing the gear, and completing 300 miles on the Tuscobia Trail in the past week, Marron returned to real life by having to now rush to St. Paul with the car. The clock ticked to 1:00 a.m. He had to be there in 5 1/2 hours.

"My brain was off" so he pulled over to sleep before reaching I-94, the 1,500 miles of interstate corridor that allows a traveler to leave Detroit and land in Billings,

Montana via Illinois, Wisconsin, Minnesota and North Dakota. Somebody knocked on his window; a guy not a cop, just checking on him. After Black River Falls on westbound I-94, "I lose the road home" and just misses his most important time cutoff: his wife's, by ten minutes, 6:40 a.m.

Marron launched a brand new element to these ultra distance events with his remarkable 300-mile double distance at the Tuscobia Trail Winter Ultras. To consider repeating these distances immediately after a race finish, while most can barely complete them and if so, can't walk so well afterward, demonstrates extraordinary mental and physical acumen.

It is a concept that is way out there in physical challenges, particularly when enduring cold, snow and pulling one's survival gear on a sled. How to handle the mental side? Hard training and a strong personal life assist, but it is far more complicated than that.

When arriving home on that Friday morning, does he hit the bed to sleep for a day? Not hardly; young son, Tepeyollotl-- whose name means "Heart of the Mountains"--played with dad all morning. "I was happy I was with him," and then at noon, "We slept three hours." Finally relaxed, holding his child, Marron embraces his accomplishment. "I feel so proud."

COOLEST AND FITTEST CITY ON EARTH
CHECKPOINT ELEVEN

"Dogs bark and the caravan moves on." Old Saying

The 2013 Arrowhead, competed less than one month after Tuscobia, became a wet snow fest. Warm temperatures brought rain changing to heavy snow burying trails, competitors, sleds, skis, bikes and the forests bearing watch over the race.

Snowbikes, whose time is much less on the trails than foot or skis, suffered a DNF rate over 50 percent. Carrying a bike in deep snow loses its attraction quickly.

Only 7 of the 42 entrants for the run made the cutoffs for a chance at making the finish. Rios won with a fast start, a lead he held when crossing in 45:40. Storkamp scored a silver finish while conserving strength for his Iditarod Invitational 350 Mile a month later across Alaska. Scotch also earned a finish, but Taylor and Marron lost the race's cutoff battle when entering the MelGeo checkpoint. On the Where's Chris Scotch blog, Scotch surmised after the 2011 event, a thought relevant to all Arrowhead years: "Arrowhead doesn't care how many times you have finished before, what kind of shape you are in, or what you have won in the past; to the Arrowhead, we are all fair game to its whims."

Scotch left Thursday morning—just after his Wednesday night finish—returning the 135 miles on the Arrowhead trail to International Falls. "After breakfast, I slipped out the front door of the Fortune Bay Casino (the host hotel) and around the back of the building to where the finish line for Arrowhead was. I slowly made my way back up the 135 miles of trail to my Jeep in (International) Falls, arriving Sunday afternoon. "

"I got the double, a double-Arrowhead," Scotch wrote. "And what a year to do it," the first to cover the out-and-back-distance for the winter ultra's master race. Two doubles, two months; Tuscobia, then Arrowhead. The previously unthinkable accomplishment conquered twice in succession.

Scotch winning 2012 Arrowhead's Ernest Shackleton Award for most time on course while making forward progress

Ken and Jackie Krueger's 2014 Arrowhead 135 looks to be a doozy. "We have over 100 race veterans returning along with a class exceeding 50 rookies. The accomplishments of our racers are amazing. For example, we have four students from the Naval Academy, numerous Iditarod finishers plus all of the course record holders along with a strong group of female racers coming back. Our winter endurance racers will represent nine countries and 24 states. International Falls, Minnesota, will be the coolest and fittest city on earth January 27, 2014."

Polfuss is deciding which Tuscobia distance to enter in 2013. With great experience at such a young age, he has potentially a long and unique future ahead in ultra distant winter ultras.

Oveson will no doubt plan to race his hometown event, International Falls' Arrowhead; the Tuscobia Trail wants him back, also. Who knows what else?

Saari, Rochester, Minn. will team with husband, ultra trail champion Daryl, to race the 150 at Tuscobia on bikes. The snowbike phenomena continues to explode in popularity for snow endurance events. Watching one glide by while covering trails on foot seems like a nice way of going, until one experiences the effort and challenge that form of locomotion demands.

The multiple Gnarly Bandit Ultra Trail Series Winner, Taylor, expects to continue conquering the winter distance events. After all, the Wilderness Athlete Gnarly Bandit is all about 100 mile distances. His plans include another entry in the 2013 Tuscobia 150.

Storkamp finished a phenomenal winter season. Starting with Tuscobia, then completing one of the most difficult years for Arrowhead, he finally raced his dream, the Iditarod Invitational completing 350 snow-miles on foot. That's 350 very difficult miles in extreme Alaskan terrain. Fully self-supported, the race brings out every emotion possible along with the very real possibility of not finishing after all of the effort and expense one endures just to make the start. One is truly at risk, too. There is no place to hide between distant aid stations, no one to come out and check on your well-being. The circus tents, bands and hoopla are back in the continental U.S.A. The Iditarod Invitational website has an introduction by Bill Merchant who sports titles of Trail Manager/Racer. He markedly points out, "We differ from other races in that we allow racers to make these decisions for themselves about what to carry, when to rest and when it is safe to travel.

There is no designated or marked route only mandatory checkpoints racers must pass through. As a race organizer it would be much less stressful to have all the rules, restrictions and support offered in other races, but as a racer I want to make and be responsible for my own decisions."

This is seriously hardcore, particularly as he talks about the risks. "A mistake at the wrong time and place in the Alaskan winter wilderness could cost you fingers and toes or even your life. At times the only possible rescue will be self rescue." Storkamp remained unperturbed. "I started to realize how isolated I truly was during the race, and how this race was only for those cable of being self-sufficient and capable of self-rescue. It really started to dawn on me that the experiences I have had as an ultrarunner and more importantly as an outdoorsman with extensive winter camping, trekking and winter racing experience over many years prepared me for the adventure that is the Iditarod 350. It was never easy, but I was never at a loss for what to do or how to take care of myself in those extreme conditions."

Asked to point out an example of taking care of one's self, he pointed out the differences of this distance when eating. "I fueled in a similar fashion, eating the same type of foods, but overall I ate a lot more." He cautioned, one can't get behind in their calories. "If you start running a deficit after the first couple of days, you will pay for it later. So, I really worked on getting the calories in, eating about 5,500 per day. You're basically always eating something." Ahh, finally uncovered . . . the similarities of ultra endurance racing to televised football viewing.

He teamed with friend and winter endurance athlete, Matt Long, for the Iditarod. "Matt Long and I have done a lot of training and racing together, had finished the Arrowhead 135 together before and generally had the same mindset going into this race of not competing and working a bit under our ability while focusing on having a great experience and making it to the finish. It was a great experience doing this race with one of my closest friends, an experience I would not trade for anything."

To explain the time in numbers doesn't truly describe the strain required to complete this distance in that environment. For the record, here it is (both started/finished together).

Started   Sunday 02.24.2013 at 2:00 p.m.
Finished   Sunday 03.03.2013 at 7:15 p.m.

Total time on trail: seven days, five hours, 15 minutes

Storkamp unknowingly reveals an insight on the mindset needed to race 635 miles of snow as he did in the winter of 2012-2013: think bigger. Storkamp's new reverie . . . accept the challenge of the 1000 mile Iditarod Trail Invitational. Think, way bigger.

Marron enters the 2013 Tuscobia 150-mile race with no intention of repeating his 2012 300 performance; he has other major distance races in mind. As a pioneer in the 150, though, he has no choice now but to continue his finisher's streak at Tuscobia's distance race; only Marron and Scotch have raced and finished every 150 held there. The racing résumé requires it; get that five-year finisher status, earn the ten-year one, too. Besides, he has other super-distance objectives in mind that he will reveal . . . later.

The Age of Aquarius reflecting the freedom, nonconformity, veracity, perseverance, and humanity of endurance athletes is now underway. The ultra-double era is pioneered with 300 miles at the 2012 Tuscobia Ultra Winter races by a quiet, shy, highly determined and imaginative Roberto Marron.

The All-American man, Chris Scotch confirms the new twist to the sport with his Arrowhead double while completing Canada's Actif Epica to achieve one of sport's most unique recognitions, the Order of the Hrimthurs. Then John Storkamp astounds by racing 635 miles on three snow events in about 60 days.

Incredibly, the sport witnesses a whole new level of athletic achievement, pain and achievement. The future of the double-super-ultra looks as endless as those starry skies Marron stared at when stretched out inside his Tuscobia sleeping bag, December 2012.

REVERIE
FINISH LINE TWELVE

"Celebrate the Spirit of Frost Giants" Order of the Hrimthurs

My own experience snowshoe racing the trails at Tuscobia taught me many things. Some of those I included in a feature for Snowshoe Magazine titled . . .

Tuscobia Winter Ultras: Top 10 Reasons NOT to Drop at Any Distance
Use this QR for article or use search

My Amazon Author's Page
Use this QR for page or use search

HARMONIZING: Keys to Living in the Song of Life
ULTRA SUPERIOR
The 300-Mile Man:
Roberto Marron Doubles Tuscobia's Winter Ultra 150

SEARCH TERMS
Superior Trail Races
Tuscobia Winter Ultras
Arrowhead 135
Actif Epica
Rock Steady Racing

Snowshoe Magazine: *www.snowshoemag.com*
Thanks to Ryan Alford, Publisher, for the permission to publish this story in this form.

The Superior 100 is one of the founding races in the ultra difficult *Wilderness Athlete's Gnarly Bandit Ultra Trail Series* hosted by the Upper Midwest Trail Runners (UMTR)

Wilderness Athlete:
The Authority on Outdoor Performance Nutrition™

One Last Thought:
Remember the words of immortal Steve Prefontaine . . . .
"Don't let fatigue make a coward of you"
Though it can . . . and does.

One Last Discovery:
Perhaps the most unique award in sports,
Celebrating the spirit of the Frost Giants:
The Order of the Hrimthurs

Photo Credits

Cover	Roberto Marron Collection
Crossing	Arrowhead 135
Frozen Faces	Arrowhead 135
1960 KE-95	Vintage Snowmobiles.50megs.com
Self	John Storkamp Collection
Self	Chuck Fritz Collection
Solitary	Tuscobia Winter Ultras
Duo	Roberto Marron Collection
Buffalo	Roberto Marron Collection
Scotch	Arrowhead 135

"Tis in grain, sir; 'twill endure wind and weather."
(Twelfth Night: I. v from William Shakespeare)

RESULTS & AUTOGRAPHS

About the Author:

Phillip Gary Smith
has spent more than 35 years as a stockbroker and in venture funding, helping finance and develop a myriad of technologies and businesses. Award-winning writing grew as a benefit of miles and time on dirt and snow trails with articles/features in Snowshoe Magazine (Senior Editor), Senior Columnist Radioactive Drag Racing News, and senior correspondent/writer for other publications. He has published two previous books. He lives in the Twin Cities with his wife, Jill. They enjoy two daughters and their husbands.

www.ingramcontent.com/pod-product-compliance
Lightning Source LLC
LaVergne TN
LVHW010028070426
835513LV00001B/16